ASSERTIVENESS TRAINING

A Guide to Empowerment

Dan Crown

Independently published

ISBN: 9798884248434

Cover design by: Dan Crown

CONTENTS

THE ART OF ASSERTIVE COMMUNICATION

In the realm of personal and professional development, mastering the art of assertive communication stands as a cornerstone of effective interaction and conflict resolution. Assertiveness, unlike aggression or passivity, allows individuals to express their thoughts, feelings, and needs in a clear, direct, and respectful manner. This chapter delves into the strategies and nuances of assertive communication, guiding you to navigate conversations with confidence and integrity.

Understanding Assertiveness

Assertiveness is the balanced midpoint on the communication spectrum, situated between passive and aggressive behaviors. It involves expressing your own rights, needs, and desires without undermining those of others. Assertiveness is rooted in self-respect and respect for others, fostering an environment of mutual understanding and respect.

Key Characteristics of Assertive Communication

Clarity and Directness: Assertive communication is straightforward and unambiguous. It conveys messages in a clear and understandable manner, leaving little room for misinterpretation.

Honesty: It involves being truthful about your thoughts and feelings while considering the situation's sensitivity and the other person's feelings.

Respect: Assertive individuals communicate with respect for both themselves and others, ensuring that the conversation maintains dignity and consideration for all parties involved.

Confidence: Assertive communicators speak with confidence, demonstrating that they value their own opinions and rights.

Strategies for Assertive Communication

I. Know Your Value

Understanding and believing in your inherent worth is the foundation of assertive communication. Recognize that your feelings, thoughts, and needs are valid and important. This self-assurance will ground your assertive expressions, making them more impactful and genuine.

II. Use "I" Statements

"I" statements allow you to express your feelings and thoughts without blaming or accusing the other person. For example, instead of saying, "You never listen to me," you might say, "I feel unheard when my ideas aren't acknowledged." This approach reduces defensiveness and opens up space for constructive dialogue.

III. Practice Active Listening

Assertiveness is not just about expressing your own needs; it's also about understanding others. Active listening involves giving your full attention, reflecting back what you've heard, and showing empathy. This creates a respectful atmosphere conducive to open and honest communication.

IV. Set Clear Boundaries

Assertive communication involves setting and respecting boundaries. Clearly define your limits and communicate them to others in a respectful yet firm manner. This helps prevent resentment and misunderstanding, ensuring that your needs and those of others are balanced.

V. Handle Criticism Constructively

Receiving criticism is an inevitable part of communication. Respond to criticism assertively by listening calmly, seeking clarity, and distinguishing between constructive feedback and personal attacks. Use it as an opportunity for growth, rather than a trigger for conflict.

VI. Practice, Practice, Practice

Developing assertiveness is a skill that requires practice. Start with low-stakes situations and gradually work your way up to more challenging conversations. Reflect on your experiences, learn from them, and continue to refine your approach.

Common Challenges and Solutions

Fear of Conflict: Many avoid assertiveness due to a fear of causing conflict. Remember, assertiveness reduces the likelihood of conflict by promoting clear and respectful communication.
Guilt: Some feel guilty for asserting their needs. It's vital to recognize that asserting yourself respectfully is a healthy and necessary part of interpersonal relationships.
Misinterpretation: Others may initially perceive your assertiveness as aggression. Consistency in respectful and clear communication will help redefine these perceptions over time.

Conclusion

The art of assertive communication is a transformative tool that empowers individuals to express themselves effectively and respectfully. By embracing the principles and strategies outlined in this chapter, you can enhance your interpersonal relationships, achieve your goals, and navigate the complexities of human interaction with grace and confidence. Assertiveness is not just a communication style; it's a pathway to a more fulfilling and respectful existence.

DAN CROWN

A GUIDE TO SELF-EMPOWERMENT

Understanding Your Patterns

To embark on a journey toward assertiveness, you must first understand your patterns of behavior and communication. Each of us has a unique style of interacting with the world, deeply influenced by our upbringing, experiences, and the coping mechanisms we've developed over time. Some may find themselves retreating into passivity when faced with conflict, while others may adopt an aggressive stance, perhaps as a defense mechanism. Then, there are those who oscillate between these extremes, exhibiting passive-aggressive behaviors as a way to express discontent without direct confrontation.

Highlighting Your Strengths and Weaknesses

Self-assessment is a powerful tool in recognizing your strengths and weaknesses. Reflect on situations where your communication style has either served you well or led to misunderstandings and conflicts. This reflection isn't about self-criticism but about acknowledging where you are and envisioning where you'd like to be. Your strengths are the foundation upon which you can build a more assertive self. Your weaknesses, on the other hand, are not flaws but areas ripe for development and growth.

DAN CROWN

Understanding Communication Styles

Passive: Passive communicators often struggle to express their needs and desires, usually out of fear of upsetting others or causing conflict. While this might seem like a way to maintain peace, it often leads to resentment and a feeling of being overlooked or undervalued.

Aggressive: Aggressive communication is characterized by an overemphasis on expressing one's own needs, often at the expense of others. It can lead to damaged relationships and a lack of mutual respect, as it prioritizes the individual's desires over collective harmony.

Passive-Aggressive: This style is marked by indirect resistance and avoidance of direct communication. Passive-aggressive communicators may agree to things in person but express their true feelings through inaction or sarcasm, leading to confusion and mistrust.

Assertive: Assertiveness is the balance between passive and aggressive styles. It involves expressing your thoughts, feelings, and needs in a clear, direct, and respectful manner. It's about standing up for yourself without trampling on others, fostering an environment of mutual respect and understanding.

Standing Up for Yourself

Standing up for yourself is at the heart of assertiveness. It means being honest about your feelings and needs, setting boundaries, and respecting others' boundaries in return. Here are steps to cultivate assertiveness:

Identify Your Needs: Clearly understand what you need from a given situation or relationship. This clarity will guide your actions and words.

Express Yourself Clearly: Use "I" statements to express your thoughts and feelings without blaming or criticizing others. For example, "I feel upset when my work is overlooked" instead of "You always ignore my contributions."

Listen Actively: Assertiveness is a two-way street. Listen to others' perspectives and respond empathetically. This shows respect for their thoughts and feelings and encourages them to reciprocate.

Practice Saying No: Learning to say no is crucial. It's about respecting your limits and not overcommitting. Remember, saying no to something can mean saying yes to your well-being.

Seek Feedback: Ask for feedback on your communication style from trusted friends, family, or colleagues. Their insights can provide valuable perspectives on your growth areas.

Self-assessment: The Foundation of Growth

Self-assessment involves regular reflection on your communication style, behaviors, and the outcomes they lead to. Consider keeping a journal to note instances where you successfully stood up for yourself and times you fell into passive, aggressive, or passive-aggressive patterns. Reflect on these entries to understand your triggers and progress.

By embracing assertiveness, you're not just advocating for yourself; you're also contributing to healthier, more respectful, and more fulfilling relationships. Assertiveness is a journey, one that requires patience, practice, and self-compassion. With each step, you're not only finding your voice but also learning the profound value of listening to others. This balance is the essence of assertiveness, a powerful tool for personal and professional growth.

EMBRACING SELF-COMPASSION

Understanding Self-Compassion and Self-Acceptance

In the journey toward assertiveness, two foundational stones are self-compassion and self-acceptance. Self-compassion involves treating yourself with the same kindness, concern, and support you would offer a good friend when they suffer, fail, or feel inadequate. It's about recognizing that suffering and personal inadequacy are part of the shared human experience. Self-acceptance goes hand in hand with self-compassion, urging you to acknowledge and accept your flaws and weaknesses as part of your human condition, without self-judgment.

The Importance of Self-Compassion in Assertiveness

Self-compassion is vital in assertiveness training because it allows us to approach our mistakes and shortcomings with kindness rather than criticism. This nurturing attitude towards oneself fosters a growth mindset, encouraging personal development and resilience. When you practice self-compassion, you are less afraid of rejection or criticism from others, as you do not base your self-worth on the approval of others. This makes it easier to express your needs, thoughts, and feelings openly and assertively.

How Self-Acceptance Fuels Assertive Behavior

Self-acceptance empowers you to recognize and accept your value as an individual, irrespective of your imperfections or the approval of others. This acknowledgment acts as a catalyst for assertive behavior, as it instills a deep-seated sense of self-worth that doesn't waver in the face of external opinions. When you accept yourself, you feel more comfortable expressing your true self, setting boundaries, and standing up for your rights and needs.

The Personal Bill of Rights

An essential tool in assertiveness training is the concept of the personal bill of rights. This is a list of rights that every individual inherently possesses, which serves as a reminder that your needs and feelings are just as important as anyone else's. Some of these rights include:

1. **The right to be treated with respect.**
2. **The right to express your feelings, opinions, and wants.**
3. **The right to set your own priorities.**
4. **The right to say 'no' without feeling guilty.**
5. **The right to make mistakes and not be perfect.**
6. **The right to follow your own values and standards.**
7. **The right to say yes because you want to, not out of obligation or to please others.**
8. **The right to be uniquely yourself.**

Understanding and embracing your personal bill of rights is crucial for assertive behavior. It serves as a constant reminder that you are entitled to respect and dignity, and it helps you to set boundaries and advocate for yourself in various situations.

Practicing Self-Compassion, Self-Acceptance, and Assertiveness

Integrating self-compassion and self-acceptance into your life requires intentional practice. Here are some strategies to get started:

Practice mindfulness: Become more aware of your thoughts and feelings without judging them. This can help you respond to yourself with kindness rather than criticism.

Challenge negative self-talk: Replace critical or negative thoughts about yourself with more positive, compassionate, and accepting ones.

Exercise your personal bill of rights: Regularly remind yourself of your inherent rights and practice standing up for them in your daily life.

Seek feedback: Constructive criticism can be a valuable tool for growth. Seek out feedback not as a validation of your worth but as a means to improve and learn.

Embrace vulnerability: Being open about your feelings and needs requires vulnerability, which is a strength. It fosters deeper connections with others and supports authentic living.

Conclusion

The path to assertiveness is paved with self-compassion and self-acceptance. By embracing your personal bill of rights, you affirm your worth and set the stage for living more openly and assertively. Remember, assertiveness is not about being aggressive or indifferent to others; it's about expressing your true self respectfully and confidently. As you cultivate these practices, you'll find that assertiveness becomes not just a skill you apply but a way of living that honors both yourself and those around you.

NAVIGATING ASSERTIVENESS: FREEDOM FROM THE FOG OF PLEASING

In the journey of personal and professional growth, mastering the art of assertiveness is akin to finding a path through a dense fog—where the fog represents the complex emotions of fear, obligation, and guilt that often entangle us in our relationships. This chapter aims to illuminate that path, guiding you to assert your needs while preserving your reputation as a compassionate and understanding individual.

The Minefield of Interpersonal and Working Relationships

Navigating the minefield of relationships requires a keen understanding of the terrain, marked by hidden pressures to conform, please, and yield to others' demands. Often, individuals fall into the role of a 'people pleaser' or 'pushover,' sacrificing their own needs and desires to avoid conflict or confrontation. This pattern, while it may offer temporary peace, ultimately leads to resentment, frustration, and a loss of self-esteem.

Freedom Through Assertiveness

Assertiveness offers a way out—a means to claim your freedom. It involves expressing your thoughts, feelings, and needs directly, honestly, and respectfully. Unlike aggression, which overpowers, or passivity, which surrenders, assertiveness respects both your rights and those of others. It's about finding your voice and standing your ground, even in the face of opposition or emotional blackmail.

The Fog of Fear, Obligation, and Guilt (FOG)

Many shy away from assertiveness, trapped in the fog of fear (of rejection or conflict), obligation (to fulfill others' expectations), and guilt (for putting oneself first). This FOG can be disorienting, blurring the lines between genuine responsibility and undue burden. Learning to navigate this fog involves recognizing these feelings for what they are—barriers to your well-being and autonomy.

Asserting Your Needs

Asserting your needs starts with acknowledging them. It's essential to understand that your needs are valid and deserve attention. This doesn't mean disregarding the needs of others but rather ensuring that your voice is heard. Techniques such as "I" statements can be instrumental in this process, allowing you to express your feelings and requests without blaming or attacking the other person.

Avoiding Emotional Blackmail

Emotional blackmail is a manipulation tactic used to exert control through fear, obligation, and guilt. Recognizing and resisting this tactic is crucial. You have the right to set boundaries and say no, even when pressured. Remember, being assertive means respecting yourself enough to protect your mental and emotional well-being.

From Avoiding Conflict to Embracing Self-Advocacy

Avoiding conflict is a natural instinct, but it often comes at the expense of your own needs and happiness. Self-advocacy is about embracing the discomfort that sometimes accompanies standing up for yourself. It involves developing the confidence to navigate confrontations constructively, without aggression or passivity.

The Trap of Seeking Approval

The desire for approval is deeply ingrained in many of us. However, an excessive need for validation can make you vulnerable to neglecting your own needs. Learning to assert yourself involves recognizing your worth independently of others' opinions or approval.

Learning to Assert

Learning to assert yourself is a skill that can be developed over time. It involves practice, patience, and sometimes stepping out of your comfort zone. Start small, with situations that feel less intimidating, and gradually build up your confidence. Remember, assertiveness is a balance—a dance between your needs and those of others.

Being assertive does not mean you have to sacrifice being seen as a nice person. On the contrary, assertiveness can enhance your relationships by fostering honesty, respect, and mutual understanding. It's about being kind but also clear and firm in your convictions. Assertiveness allows you to be genuinely nice, not out of obligation or fear, but out of a strong sense of self-respect and respect for others.

In conclusion, **stepping out of the fog of pleasing others to assert your needs is a profound act of self-liberation**. It empowers you to navigate the minefield of relationships with confidence, preserving your well-being and dignity. As you journey through this process, remember that assertiveness is not just a skill but a gateway to genuine freedom and fulfillment in your interpersonal and working relationships.

THE ART OF ASSERTIVENESS - EMBRACING THE POWER OF "NO"

In the journey of assertiveness training, one of the most crucial skills to master is the ability to say "No" without tension. This chapter delves into practical strategies and psychological underpinnings that empower you to navigate mini confrontations, shift your language from "I can't" to "I don't", and examine your beliefs around saying no. By integrating these techniques into your daily interactions, you'll not only bolster your assertiveness but also enhance your personal and professional relationships.

Saying No Without Tension

The act of saying "No" often brings a sense of tension, guilt, or fear of offending others. However, asserting your boundaries is a vital aspect of self-respect and respect for others. The key to saying no without tension lies in the realization that you have a right to your preferences, needs, and time. Practice saying "No" in a calm and firm tone, without over-explaining your reasons. This straightforward approach reduces the tension for both parties, making it clear that your decision isn't personal but rather a matter of personal choice or capacity.

Embrace Mini Confrontations

Mini confrontations are inevitable when you start asserting your boundaries. Rather than avoiding them, view these moments as opportunities for growth and clarification. A mini confrontation doesn't have to be a full-blown conflict; it can simply be a moment where you stand your ground in a respectful manner. Use these instances to practice calmness, clarity, and the art of disagreement without hostility. Remember, assertiveness isn't about winning an argument but about expressing your needs and perspectives honestly and respectfully.

Shift from "I Can't" to "I Don't"

Language plays a pivotal role in how we perceive and are perceived by others. The transition from saying "I can't" to "I don't" is a powerful linguistic shift that reflects a stronger sense of agency and personal choice. "I can't" often sounds like an excuse and may imply that under different circumstances, you might say yes. On the other hand, "I don't" signals a clear and deliberate choice, rooted in your values or priorities. For instance, "I don't check emails after 6 pm" comes across as a personal policy rather than a temporary inability.

Examine Your Beliefs Around Saying No

Our difficulty with saying "No" often stems from deep-seated beliefs about the need to be liked, to please others, or fears of being perceived as selfish. To move past these barriers, it's essential to examine and challenge these beliefs. Reflect on the following questions:

- Why do I feel guilty about saying no?

- What am I afraid will happen if I say no?
- Do I believe that my needs are as important as others'?

By confronting these beliefs, you can begin to dismantle the guilt or fear associated with saying no. Realize that saying no is not just about rejecting a request but about honoring your capacity, values, and priorities.

Conclusion

Mastering the art of saying "No" is a cornerstone of assertiveness training. By learning to say no without tension, embracing mini confrontations, shifting your language, and examining your underlying beliefs, you cultivate a sense of empowerment and respect in your interactions. Remember, being assertive is not about being unkind or inflexible; it's about communicating your needs and boundaries clearly and respectfully. As you integrate these practices into your life, you'll find that assertiveness becomes not just a skill but a way of living that respects both yourself and others.

EMBRACING SELF-PRIORITIZATION AND COMPASSION

In the journey towards becoming more assertive, the principles of self-prioritization, self-compassion, self-acceptance, and recognizing your personal bill of rights stand as foundational pillars. This chapter delves into how these concepts interlace with assertiveness, empowering you to communicate your needs and boundaries effectively while nurturing your well-being.

Self-Prioritization: The First Step to Assertiveness

Self-prioritization is not about selfishness; it's about recognizing the importance of your well-being and needs. It's understanding that for you to be of service to others, you need to be in a state of balance and fulfillment yourself. Prioritizing yourself means giving yourself permission to assess what you need, whether it's time, space, or specific resources, and then taking steps to meet those needs.

The practice of self-prioritization involves:

Time Management: Allocate time for activities that nourish your body, mind, and soul. It could be exercise, reading, or pursuing a hobby.

Setting Boundaries: Clearly define what is acceptable and unacceptable in your interactions with others. Boundaries protect your energy and well-being.

Saying No: Learn to decline requests that conflict with your priorities or well-being. Saying no is a powerful assertiveness tool.

Self-Compassion: Your Assertiveness Companion

Self-compassion is treating yourself with the same kindness, concern, and support you'd offer a good friend. When embarking on assertiveness, you'll encounter challenges and possibly setbacks. Self-compassion encourages you to be gentle with yourself during these times, recognizing that perfection is not the goal; growth is.

Practicing self-compassion involves:

Mindfulness: Observe your thoughts and feelings without judgment. Acknowledge your feelings, understand them, and then move forward with purpose.

Kindness: Replace self-criticism with positive affirmations and encouragement. Speak to yourself as you would to someone you care deeply about.

Common Humanity: Understand that you're not alone in your struggles. Everyone faces challenges, and it's part of the human experience.

Self-Acceptance: The Foundation of Your Assertive Voice

Self-acceptance means acknowledging and embracing all aspects of yourself—your strengths, weaknesses, achievements, and failures. It's recognizing that your worth isn't based on external validations or successes but on your intrinsic value as a person.

To foster self-acceptance:

Reflect on Your Achievements: Regularly remind yourself of your accomplishments and strengths.

Forgive Yourself: Let go of past mistakes and view them as learning opportunities.

Celebrate Your Uniqueness: Embrace your individuality and the qualities that make you, you.

Your Personal Bill of Rights: Asserting Your Worth

Understanding your personal bill of rights is crucial in assertiveness training. It's a set of principles that affirm your rights in your relationships with others. These rights include the freedom to express your feelings, to say no without feeling guilty, to be treated with respect, to make your needs as important as others', and to be accepting of your mistakes and failures.

Your personal bill of rights serves as a reminder that your needs and feelings are valid and important. It's a declaration of your worth and dignity.

Conclusion

The path to assertiveness is paved with the practices of self-prioritization, self-compassion, self-acceptance, and embracing your personal bill of rights. These principles not only enhance your assertiveness skills but also contribute to a more balanced and fulfilling life. Remember, being assertive means respecting yourself enough to express your needs and boundaries while respecting others. By integrating these principles into your daily life, you'll find that assertiveness becomes not just a skill, but a natural extension of your respect for yourself and others.

MOVING BEYOND THE NEED TO PLEASE: CULTIVATING ASSERTIVENESS

In the journey toward assertiveness, understanding the deep-rooted desire to please others is a critical step. This chapter delves into the complex interplay between the need to please, agreeableness, and the importance of enforcing personal boundaries. By addressing these key areas, we aim to empower individuals to cultivate a more assertive stance in life, one that honors both their needs and the respect for others.

The Allure of Being Accommodating

Being accommodating and agreeable has its roots in a natural human desire for social harmony and approval. Agreeableness, as a personality trait, reflects a person's tendency to be kind, cooperative, and sympathetic towards others. On the surface, these qualities are commendable and can foster positive relationships. However, when the desire to be agreeable morphs into compulsive people-pleasing, it can lead to self-neglect and resentment.

The Pitfalls of People-Pleasing

People-pleasing is an attempt to secure love and approval by constantly putting others' needs before one's own. This behavior pattern can lead to being perceived as a pushover, someone who is easily swayed or exploited due to their inability to say no. The primary issue with people-pleasing is not the act of helping others but the underlying fear of rejection and the loss of approval that drives it.

Enforcing Your Boundaries

Enforcing personal boundaries is a crucial aspect of moving away from people-pleasing behaviors. Boundaries allow us to define what we are comfortable with and how we wish to be treated by others. They are essential for maintaining self-respect and preventing burnout. However, for many, the thought of setting boundaries evokes fear of conflict or the loss of relationships.

Strategies for Cultivating Assertiveness

1. **Recognize the Need to Please**: Begin by acknowledging the behaviors and motivations behind your people-pleasing tendencies. Understanding why you feel compelled to please can help in addressing the root causes.

2. **Define Your Boundaries**: Clearly define your limits and non-negotiables. Understand that boundaries are not about controlling others but about respecting yourself.

3. **Practice Saying No:** Start with small, low-stakes situations to build your confidence in refusing requests. Remember, saying no does not make you unkind or selfish; it signifies respect for your needs and time.

4. **Seek Approval from Within:** Shift the focus from seeking

external validation to nurturing self-approval. Engage in self-reflection and celebrate your achievements and qualities, irrespective of others' opinions.

5. Communicate Assertively: Assertive communication involves expressing your thoughts and feelings openly and respectfully. Use "I" statements to own your experiences without blaming or attacking others.

6. Manage Guilt and Anxiety: Feeling guilty or anxious after asserting yourself is common. Recognize these feelings as part of the process and remind yourself of the importance of your well-being.

7. Seek Support: Surround yourself with people who respect your boundaries and encourage your growth. A supportive community can provide strength and validation as you navigate this journey.

Conclusion

Overcoming the need to please and cultivating assertiveness is not about disregarding the needs of others but about finding a balanced approach to interpersonal relationships. It involves honoring your needs and expressing them with confidence and respect. By embracing assertiveness, you not only enhance your own well-being but also contribute to healthier, more honest relationships. Remember, assertiveness is a skill that can be developed over time with practice, patience, and persistence.

THE BALANCE OF ASSERTIVENESS THROUGH MASLOW'S HIERARCHY OF NEEDS

Assertiveness is a skill that many strive to develop, a middle ground between passive and aggressive behavior. It involves expressing one's opinions, needs, and boundaries clearly and respectfully, without infringing on the rights of others. Understanding the balance of assertiveness requires a deep dive into human motivation and behavior, for which Abraham Maslow's hierarchy of needs provides a perfect framework.

Understanding Maslow's Hierarchy of Needs

Maslow's hierarchy of needs is a psychological theory that categorizes human needs into five levels: physiological, safety, love/belonging, esteem, and self-actualization. According to Maslow, these needs follow a sequence. One must satisfy lower-level needs before addressing higher-level needs.

Applying Maslow to Assertiveness

Assertiveness is not just a communication skill; it is also deeply tied to our psychological needs. Let's explore how each level of

Maslow's hierarchy relates to assertiveness:

1. Physiological Needs: At the most basic level, assertiveness can help individuals advocate for their needs for food, shelter, and health. For example, negotiating a fair salary ensures you can provide for your basic needs.

2. Safety Needs: Once physiological needs are met, the focus shifts to safety. Assertiveness plays a crucial role in establishing a safe environment, whether it's advocating for safe working conditions or setting boundaries in relationships to protect emotional well-being.

3. Love and Belonging: This level focuses on relationships and social connections. Assertiveness is key to forming healthy, balanced relationships. It allows individuals to express their needs and desires while respecting others, fostering a sense of belonging and mutual respect.

4. Esteem Needs: Esteem needs involve respect, self-esteem, and recognition. Assertiveness helps individuals pursue achievements and gain recognition without resorting to aggression or passivity. It empowers one to seek opportunities, ask for feedback, and stand up against unfair treatment.

5. Self-Actualization: The pinnacle of Maslow's hierarchy is the realization of one's full potential. Assertiveness is a crucial skill at this level, as it enables individuals to pursue their goals, express their creativity, and make choices that align with their values and aspirations.

The Balance of Assertiveness

Balancing assertiveness involves understanding and respecting your own needs and those of others. It means recognizing which level of Maslow's hierarchy you are addressing and adjusting your assertive communication to meet those needs effectively. It's about self-awareness, empathy, and the ability to navigate different social situations.

For instance, when discussing a promotion, understanding your esteem needs can guide your approach to the conversation. Recognizing the other person's potential safety and esteem needs can help you frame your request in a way that is assertive yet respectful of their position and constraints.

Practical Steps for Developing Assertive Behavior

1. Self-Reflection: Regularly assess which of Maslow's needs you're striving to meet and how assertiveness can help you achieve them.

2. Empathy: Try to understand the needs of others before you communicate. This can help you tailor your message for a more positive reception.

3. Practice: Assertiveness is a skill that improves with practice. Start with low-stakes situations and gradually work your way up as you become more comfortable.

4. Feedback: Seek feedback on your assertiveness from trusted friends, family, or mentors. They can provide valuable insights into your communication style.

Conclusion

The balance of assertiveness is about harmoniously advocating for our needs while respecting those of others, guided by an understanding of Maslow's hierarchy of needs. By practicing assertiveness within this framework, individuals can navigate their way towards fulfilling relationships and personal growth, achieving a sense of well-being and self-actualization.

UNDERSTANDING YOUR PATTERNS IN ASSERTIVENESS

Assertiveness is not just a skill; it's a practice that intertwines deeply with your behavioral patterns and psychological makeup. This chapter delves into the importance of understanding your own patterns when it comes to communication and interaction with others. By dissecting these patterns, you'll be better equipped to cultivate assertiveness in your daily life.

The Foundation of Patterns

Every individual possesses unique patterns of behavior that dictate how they respond to various situations. These patterns are often ingrained through years of experiences and can significantly influence our ability to communicate assertively. Understanding your patterns requires a deep dive into your reactions, emotions, and thoughts in different scenarios.

Identify Your Triggers: Begin by identifying situations that trigger non-assertive behavior. Is it a particular person, a specific type of request, or maybe a certain environment? Recognizing these triggers is the first step in understanding your patterns.

Analyze Your Responses: Once you've identified your triggers, reflect on how you typically respond. Do you withdraw, become aggressive, or perhaps acquiesce too readily? Understanding these responses provides insight into your default patterns of behavior.

The Impact of Emotional Responses

Emotions play a critical role in how we communicate. Assertiveness requires managing our emotional responses so they don't hinder our ability to express ourselves clearly and respectfully.

Emotional Awareness: Cultivate an awareness of your emotions. When you feel a strong emotional reaction, take a moment to acknowledge it without judgment. This awareness can help you choose a more assertive response instead of reacting impulsively.

Practice Emotional Regulation: Techniques such as deep breathing, mindfulness, and positive self-talk can help regulate your emotions in the heat of the moment, allowing you to maintain assertiveness even when challenged.

Cognitive Patterns and Assertiveness

Our thoughts and beliefs about ourselves and others can significantly impact our ability to be assertive. Negative self-talk and limiting beliefs can undermine our confidence and hinder assertive communication.

Challenge Negative Thoughts: Identify and challenge any negative thoughts or beliefs that may be holding you back. Replace them with more positive, empowering beliefs that support assertive behavior.

Adopt a Growth Mindset: Embrace the belief that you can develop and improve your assertiveness skills over time. This mindset encourages resilience and persistence in the face of challenges.

Behavioral Changes for Assertiveness

Changing ingrained patterns of behavior requires conscious effort and practice. Here are strategies to help integrate assertive behavior into your daily interactions:

Start Small: Begin with small, low-stakes situations where you can practice assertiveness without too much pressure. Gradually, as your confidence grows, tackle more challenging situations.

Use Assertive Language: Pay attention to your language. Use "I" statements to express your feelings and needs without blaming or criticizing others. Practice being clear, concise, and respectful in your communication.

Set Boundaries: Understand your limits and communicate them clearly to others. Setting and maintaining boundaries is a key component of assertive behavior.

Seek Feedback: Ask for feedback from trusted friends or colleagues about your assertiveness. This can provide valuable insights into your progress and areas for improvement.

In Conclusion

Understanding your patterns is crucial to developing assertiveness. It involves recognizing your triggers, managing your emotional responses, challenging negative cognitive patterns, and making behavioral changes. With time and practice, you can break free from non-assertive habits and embrace a more confident, assertive way of communicating. Remember, assertiveness is a journey, not a destination. Be patient and persistent, and celebrate your progress along the way.

BEYOND THE NEED TO PLEASE

In our journey through life, we often encounter the intrinsic desire to be liked and approved of by others. This need to please can manifest in consistently agreeable and accommodating behavior, leading us to set aside our own needs, desires, and boundaries in favor of others'. While being kind and considerate is undoubtedly valuable, an overemphasis on people-pleasing can hinder our ability to take control of our own lives. This chapter delves into the heart of assertiveness training, providing strategies to balance kindness with self-assurance, thereby enabling you to become comfortable with confrontation when necessary.

Understanding the Need to Please

The need to please is rooted in our evolutionary desire for social cohesion and acceptance. However, in modern contexts, this can translate into a perpetual cycle of seeking validation through agreeableness, often at the expense of our own well-being. Recognizing this pattern is the first step towards cultivating a healthier self-image that doesn't rely exclusively on others' approval.

The Role of Boundaries

Boundaries are the cornerstone of assertiveness. They define where we end and others begin, outlining what we are comfortable with, how we wish to be treated, and what we are willing to tolerate. Establishing clear boundaries is not an act of selfishness; rather, it's a declaration of self-respect and a crucial step in taking control of your own life.

Identify Your Boundaries: Reflect on situations where you felt uncomfortable, resentful, or taken advantage of. These emotions often indicate where boundaries need to be established.
Communicate Your Boundaries: Once you've identified your boundaries, the next step is to communicate them clearly, respectfully, and assertively to others.

Overcoming the Fear of Confrontation

Many of us equate confrontation with conflict, viewing it as inherently negative. However, confrontation is merely a tool for expressing our needs and addressing issues before they escalate. Becoming comfortable with confrontation involves reframing it as an opportunity for growth and understanding.

Start Small: Practice expressing your needs in low-stakes situations to build your confidence.
Use "I" Statements: Frame your concerns from your perspective to avoid blaming or accusing others, which can escalate tensions.
Stay Calm and Respectful: Maintaining composure and respect during confrontation encourages constructive dialogue.

Strategies for Assertive Living

1. **Practice Self-Reflection**: Regularly assess your actions and decisions to ensure they align with your values and needs, not just the desires of others.
2. **Learn to Say No:** Saying no is a powerful tool in maintaining

your boundaries and prioritizing your well-being.

3. Seek Balance: Strive for a balance between being accommodating and assertive. It's about finding the middle ground where your needs and the needs of others are both considered.

4. Develop Emotional Intelligence: Understanding your emotions and those of others can help in navigating interpersonal dynamics assertively.

5. Cultivate Self-Esteem: Building a strong sense of self-worth makes it easier to act assertively, as you value your own needs and opinions.

Moving Forward

Transforming from a people-pleaser to an assertive individual doesn't happen overnight. It requires patience, practice, and perseverance. Remember, assertiveness is not about winning every confrontation or always getting your way; it's about expressing yourself openly and respectfully, regardless of the outcome. By taking control of your own life and respecting your boundaries, you pave the way for more genuine, balanced, and fulfilling relationships.

FROM PEOPLE-PLEASING TO SELF-EMPOWERMENT

Embracing Assertiveness

In a world where the need to please seems embedded in our cultural fabric, many find themselves trapped in a cycle of agreeableness and accommodation. This chapter is a guide to breaking free from the shackles of people-pleasing, setting firm boundaries, and taking control of your own life. It's about becoming comfortable with confrontation—not as a means to conflict, but as a pathway to genuine assertiveness.

The Need to Please

The urge to be agreeable and accommodating often stems from a deep-seated fear of rejection or conflict. It's a survival mechanism, a way to fit in and avoid standing out for the "wrong" reasons. However, this need to please everyone can lead to a loss of self-identity and personal dissatisfaction. Recognizing this pattern is the first step toward change. Ask yourself: Whose life am I living? The answer should be yours and yours alone.

Understanding Boundaries

Boundaries are the mental, emotional, and physical limits we set to protect ourselves. They are not walls, but rather guidelines that help us respect our needs and feelings. Establishing boundaries is crucial in moving away from being overly accommodating. It sends a clear message about what you are and are not willing to tolerate. Remember, setting boundaries is not selfish; it's necessary for your well-being.

The Transition to Assertiveness

Assertiveness is the balance between aggression and passivity. It's the ability to express your feelings, needs, and desires openly and honestly, while still respecting the rights of others. The journey from people-pleasing to assertiveness requires practice and patience. Start small: express your preference for something as simple as choosing a restaurant. Gradually, you'll build the confidence to tackle more significant issues.

Taking Control of Your Own Life

Taking control means making decisions that align with your values, needs, and desires. It's about living authentically and not allowing others to dictate your life's direction. This doesn't mean disregarding the feelings or needs of others but rather not letting them overshadow your own. Empower yourself by acknowledging that you have the right to prioritize your well-being.

Becoming Comfortable with Confrontation

Many equate confrontation with conflict, but it doesn't have to be contentious. Confrontation can be a constructive discussion where differing needs or opinions are expressed healthily. The key is in the approach: be calm, clear, and respectful. Use "I" statements to express how you feel and what you need without blaming or attacking the other person. Practice active listening, showing that you value the other's perspective even as you assert your own.

Practical Steps Forward

1. **Self-reflection**: Identify areas where you tend to people-please. Understand the motivations behind these behaviors.
2. **Set Boundaries:** Start setting small boundaries. Communicate them clearly to others.
3. **Assertive Communication:** Practice stating your needs and desires openly. Use "I" statements and be respectful.
4. **Accept Discomfort**: Recognize that discomfort is part of the process. Growth occurs outside your comfort zone.
5. **Seek Support:** Surround yourself with people who respect your boundaries and encourage your assertiveness.

NAVIGATING ASSERTIVENESS: STRATEGIES FOR EFFECTIVE COMMUNICATION

In the journey towards mastering assertiveness, understanding how to navigate complex interpersonal dynamics is crucial. This chapter focuses on pivotal strategies that empower you to communicate effectively while maintaining respect and understanding. We'll explore the importance of avoiding unnecessary conflict, assuming flexibility, sticking to the facts, and avoiding the trap of over-apologizing.

The Art of Peaceful Assertiveness

Conflict avoidance doesn't mean suppressing your feelings or conceding to others unjustly; it means choosing battles wisely and aiming for peaceful resolutions. The key to assertive communication is to express your needs and opinions in a way that respects both your rights and those of others. To avoid conflict:

Practice Active Listening: Show others that you value their perspectives. Acknowledge their feelings and viewpoints without immediately jumping to conclusions or defense.

Express Your Needs Clearly: Use "I" statements to express your thoughts and feelings without blaming or criticizing the other party. For example, "I feel overlooked when my contributions aren't acknowledged" instead of "You never notice what I do."

Assume Flexibility: The Strength in Adaptability

Assertiveness is not about rigidity. Assuming flexibility means recognizing that there are multiple valid viewpoints and solutions to a problem. It's about being open to negotiation and compromise where appropriate. This approach fosters a collaborative environment, where solutions are reached through mutual respect and understanding.

Be Open to Compromise: Sometimes, the best solution is one that partially satisfies both parties. Be willing to adjust your requests or expectations to reach a mutually beneficial outcome.

Adapt Your Communication Style: Different situations and people may require different approaches. Tailor your communication style to the context and the individual you're dealing with, without compromising your values or needs.

Stick to the Facts: Building a Foundation of Trust

Assertive communication is most effective when it is grounded in reality. Sticking to the facts helps to avoid misunderstandings and keeps the conversation focused on tangible issues rather than personal attacks.

Avoid Exaggerations: Statements like "You always..." or "You never..." are not only factually incorrect but also likely to provoke defensiveness. Focus on specific instances and behaviors.

Provide Evidence: When discussing issues, refer to concrete examples and outcomes. This helps clarify your perspective and provides a solid basis for discussion.

Over-Apologizing: Asserting Without Diminishing

A common pitfall in striving to be polite is over-apologizing, which can undermine your assertiveness and make you appear less confident. It's important to distinguish between situations where an apology is warranted and those where a simple acknowledgment or alternative expression would be more appropriate.

Recognize When to Apologize: Offer apologies for your mistakes or when you've wronged someone. However, avoid apologizing for expressing your feelings, needs, or opinions.
Use Alternative Phrases: *Instead of saying "I'm sorry" for things that don't warrant an apology, try phrases like "Thank you for your patience" or "I appreciate your understanding." This allows you to acknowledge the situation without diminishing your stance.*

Conclusion

Mastering assertiveness is a journey that requires practice, reflection, and a willingness to adapt. By avoiding unnecessary conflict, assuming flexibility, sticking to the facts, and avoiding over-apologizing, you can communicate your needs and opinions effectively and respectfully. Remember, the goal of assertiveness is not to win every conversation but to express yourself honestly and respectfully, fostering healthy and productive relationships.

THE ART OF MAKING REQUESTS

In the journey of developing assertiveness, understanding how to make requests is fundamental. The way we ask for what we need or want can significantly impact the outcome. This chapter is dedicated to mastering the art of making requests with clarity, respect, and effectiveness. By incorporating the principles of specificity, offering clear options, directness, honesty, and consideration for the other person's needs, we can transform our interactions in a positive way. Additionally, we will explore how to avoid the pitfalls of passive-aggressive behavior, ensuring our communication is both respectful and straightforward.

Be Specific

When making a request, vagueness is the enemy of action. Specificity acts as a guide, providing clear direction to the person you're asking something of. For example, instead of saying, "I need help with the project," say, "Could you review the budget section of our project by tomorrow afternoon?" The latter leaves no room for ambiguity, setting clear expectations and making it easier for the person to fulfill the request.

Offer Clear Options

Offering options empowers the other person to choose how they can best assist you while respecting their autonomy. However, these options should be clear and concrete. For instance, if you're asking for assistance with a task, you might say, "Would you be able to help me with the data analysis or review the final report?" This approach shows you value their input and are flexible in how they can provide support.

Be Direct and Honest

Assertiveness is rooted in directness and honesty. Beating around the bush or hinting at what you want often leads to misunderstandings and frustration. Directly stating your needs shows confidence and respect for both yourself and the person you're communicating with. Honesty also fosters trust, an essential component of any healthy relationship. If you need something to be done because it's important for a deadline, express that urgency truthfully.

Consider the Other Person's Needs

Assertive communication is not about being selfish; it's about finding a balance between your needs and the needs of others. When making a request, take a moment to consider how it might impact the person you're asking. If your request could inconvenience them, acknowledge that and express your appreciation for their help. For example, "I realize this is short notice and might disrupt your plans, but your expertise would be invaluable for resolving this issue."

Make It Easy and Convenient

Whenever possible, make fulfilling your request as easy and convenient for the other person as you can. This might involve providing all the necessary information, materials, or support they might need to help you. By reducing the effort required on their part, you not only show consideration for their time and resources but also increase the likelihood of a positive response.

Avoiding Passive-Aggressive Behavior

A passive-aggressive approach to making requests often stems from a desire to avoid direct conflict, but it can lead to confusion, resentment, and unresolved issues. Signs of passive-aggressive behavior include making indirect requests, using sarcasm, or expressing grievances through humor. Instead, strive for open and honest communication. If you're feeling frustrated or disappointed, express those feelings directly and constructively, focusing on finding a solution rather than assigning blame.

In Practice

Imagine you need a colleague to provide feedback on a document by a specific deadline. Here's how you could apply the principles outlined in this chapter:

Specific Request: "Could you review the financial analysis section of the document by Wednesday noon?"

Offer Clear Options: "Would it be easier for you to provide feedback via comments in the document or to discuss it in a brief meeting?"

Be Direct and Honest: "Your feedback is crucial for me to finalize the document on time for the client's review."

Consider Their Needs: "I understand this is a busy week for you, so if there's anything I can do to make reviewing this quicker, please let me know."

Make It Easy: "I've highlighted the specific sections where your expertise is most needed, and I'm available for any questions you might have while reviewing."

By integrating these strategies into your request-making process, you can foster more positive, productive, and respectful interactions in both your personal and professional life. Remember, assertiveness is about clear, honest, and respectful communication. It's a skill that benefits everyone involved, paving the way for mutual understanding and cooperation.

ASSERTIVE COMMUNICATION IN THE FAMILY

In the heart of family dynamics lies communication, the cornerstone that shapes relationships, resolves conflicts, and fosters an environment of mutual respect and understanding. Among various communication styles, assertive communication stands out as the most effective, yet it is often misunderstood or underutilized within family settings. This chapter delves into the essence of assertive communication, contrasting it with passive, aggressive, and passive-aggressive styles, and unveils the profound benefits it brings to family interactions.

Understanding Communication Styles

Communication within a family can manifest in several ways, each with distinct characteristics and impacts:

Passive Communication involves avoiding expression of thoughts, feelings, or needs, often leading to misunderstandings and unmet needs within the family.
Aggressive Communication is characterized by expressing needs and emotions in a way that violates the rights of others, resulting in hurt feelings and damaged relationships.

Passive-Aggressive Communication is a covert way of expressing anger or resentment without directly acknowledging it, creating an atmosphere of mistrust and resentment.

Assertive Communication, however, strikes a balance, allowing individuals to express their thoughts, feelings, and needs openly and respectfully, fostering an environment of transparency and mutual respect.

The Benefits of Assertive Communication in the Family

Adopting assertive communication transforms family dynamics by enhancing mutual respect, encouraging honesty, reducing conflicts, and building stronger, more resilient relationships. It supports the emotional health and well-being of all family members, providing a foundation for a nurturing and supportive home environment.

Barriers to Assertive Communication

Several factors can hinder the practice of assertive communication in families, including cultural norms, upbringing, fear of conflict, and low self-esteem. Overcoming these barriers requires awareness, understanding, and a commitment to change.

Developing Assertive Communication Skills

To foster assertive communication within the family, several skills are essential:

Self-awareness is crucial for recognizing one's own communication style and its impact on others.

Empathy involves understanding and considering the feelings and needs of family members.

Clear Expression means articulating thoughts, feelings, and needs in a direct yet respectful manner.

Active Listening requires full attention to the speaker, offering empathy and understanding without immediate judgment or advice.

Setting Boundaries involves establishing personal limits respectfully and understandingly.

Practical Strategies for Families

Implementing assertive communication within a family can be facilitated through practical strategies such as role-playing, family meetings, conflict resolution techniques, and encouraging feedback. These activities not only enhance communication skills but also strengthen the bonds between family members.

Overcoming Challenges

Resistance from family members accustomed to different communication styles, managing high-emotion situations, and adjusting strategies for different age groups are common challenges. Addressing these requires patience, persistence, and sometimes professional guidance.

Conclusion

Embracing assertive communication within the family can profoundly impact relationships, creating a more open, respectful, and loving environment. It is a journey of growth, learning, and connection, requiring commitment from all family members but offering invaluable rewards in strengthened bonds and improved emotional well-being.

ASSERTIVE COMMUNICATION WITH DIFFICULT RELATIVES

Assertive communication is a key skill when dealing with difficult relatives. It allows you to express yourself clearly and respectfully, even in the face of disagreement or conflict. This chapter will guide you through the nuances of assertive communication, offering practical advice and strategies to handle challenging family dynamics effectively.

Understanding Assertiveness

Assertiveness is about expressing your thoughts, feelings, and needs in a straightforward and respectful manner. It's a middle ground between passive and aggressive communication, embodying respect for both yourself and others. When you communicate assertively, you advocate for your needs while considering the rights and feelings of those you're interacting with.

The Importance of Self-awareness

Begin with introspection. Understand your feelings, triggers, and the outcomes you desire from interactions with difficult relatives. Recognizing your emotional responses and the reasons behind them is the first step toward controlling them. This self-awareness will enable you to approach conversations with clarity and composure.

Techniques for Assertive Communication

1. Use "I" Statements: Instead of saying "You always ignore my opinions," try *"I feel disregarded when my opinions aren't considered."* This shifts the focus from blaming to expressing how you feel, reducing the likelihood of defensiveness.

2. Active Listening: Show genuine interest in the other person's perspective. Listen without interrupting, summarize what you've heard, and respond thoughtfully. This demonstrates respect and willingness to understand, paving the way for open dialogue.

3. Set Clear Boundaries: Clearly articulate your limits. If a relative frequently borrows money without returning it, you might say, "I'm happy to help in emergencies, but I cannot lend money anymore." Setting boundaries protects your well-being and communicates your expectations.

4. Practice Empathy: Try to understand where your relative is coming from. Acknowledging their feelings or viewpoint does not mean you agree, but it shows respect and consideration for their experience.

5. Stay Calm and Composed: Emotional control is crucial. If you feel overwhelmed, take a moment to breathe or ask to continue the conversation later. Responding in anger or frustration can escalate the situation.

6. Be Direct but Kind: Assertiveness does not mean being harsh. Express your needs and feelings honestly but do so with kindness and respect.

7. Agree to Disagree: Recognize that it's okay to have differing opinions. If a consensus can't be reached, respectfully agreeing to disagree can prevent unnecessary conflict.

Handling Pushback

When you start communicating assertively, some relatives might react negatively, especially if they're used to you being more passive or accommodating. Consistency is key. Remain firm in your approach, and over time, they will likely adjust to the new dynamics. Remember, you cannot control others' reactions, but you can control how you respond.

Practice Makes Progress

Developing assertive communication skills takes time and practice. Start with less challenging situations and gradually work your way up to more difficult conversations. Reflect on each interaction, noting what worked and what could be improved.

Conclusion

Dealing with difficult relatives requires patience, empathy, and assertiveness. By practicing assertive communication, you can build healthier, more respectful relationships, even in challenging family dynamics. Remember, the goal is not to win every argument but to express yourself honestly and respectfully, fostering an environment where everyone feels heard and valued.

CULTIVATING ASSERTIVENESS IN THE WORKPLACE

In the modern workplace, where collaboration and communication are pivotal, assertiveness emerges as a fundamental skill for both personal and professional growth. Assertiveness is the balanced expression of one's thoughts, feelings, and needs without infringing on the rights of others. It's about being forthright about your wants and needs, while also considering the perspectives and needs of your colleagues. This chapter delves into the art of cultivating assertiveness at work, offering practical strategies to navigate workplace dynamics with confidence and poise.

Understanding Assertiveness

Assertiveness is often misunderstood as aggression, but there's a clear distinction. Aggression disregards the rights and feelings of others, while assertiveness respects them. It's a middle ground between passive and aggressive behaviors, enabling you to stand up for yourself without stepping on others.

The Importance of Being Assertive

Being assertive at work can lead to numerous benefits, including:

Enhanced Communication: Clear and direct communication reduces misunderstandings and builds stronger relationships.

Increased Confidence: Assertiveness breeds confidence as you learn to voice your thoughts and feelings openly.

Improved Decision-Making: Assertive individuals can contribute more effectively to team decisions by offering their viewpoints.

Stress Reduction: By expressing your needs and setting boundaries, you can mitigate workplace stress and avoid resentment.

Strategies to Cultivate Assertiveness

1. Self-Reflection: Begin by understanding your own communication style. Reflect on instances where you felt your response was passive, aggressive, or assertive. Recognizing these patterns is the first step toward change.

2. Practice Clear Communication: Assertiveness is rooted in clarity. Practice being concise and direct with your words. Avoid ambiguous language and be specific about what you need or want.

3. Learn to Say No: Saying no is a powerful assertiveness tool. It involves understanding your limits and respecting them. Remember, saying no allows you to say yes to tasks and responsibilities that align with your priorities and capacities.

4. Use "I" Statements: Express your feelings and needs from your perspective to avoid sounding accusatory. For example, instead of saying, "You always disregard my ideas," try, "I feel undervalued when my ideas aren't considered."

5. Assertive Body Language: Non-verbal cues are as important as verbal ones. Maintain eye contact, stand or sit straight, and use gestures that convey confidence without aggressiveness.

6. Practice Active Listening: Assertiveness is a two-way street.

Listen actively to others, showing respect for their opinions and feelings. This fosters mutual respect and understanding.

7. Set Boundaries: Clearly define your limits and communicate them respectfully. Boundaries help others understand your expectations and how best to interact with you.

8. Seek Feedback: After attempting assertive communication, seek feedback from trusted colleagues or mentors. This can provide insights into how your efforts are perceived and areas for improvement.

9. Handle Criticism Positively: View criticism as an opportunity for growth. Respond to it assertively, seeking clarification and ways to improve.

Overcoming Barriers to Assertiveness

Common barriers include fear of conflict, desire to please, and lack of self-esteem. Overcoming these barriers requires practice, patience, and sometimes, support from mentors or professional development programs. Remember, assertiveness is a skill developed over time, not overnight.

In Conclusion

Cultivating assertiveness in the workplace is a journey towards better communication, stronger relationships, and increased job satisfaction. By practicing the strategies outlined in this chapter, you can navigate workplace dynamics more effectively, contributing to a healthier, more productive work environment. Assertiveness is not just about speaking up; it's about doing so in a way that respects both you and those around you.

THE ART OF ASSERTIVE BODY LANGUAGE

In the realm of communication, the words we choose carry significant weight, but the silent signals we send through our body language are equally powerful, if not more so. Assertive communication is not just about what we say but also about how we say it. This chapter delves into the nuances of assertive body language, offering insights and practical advice to help you convey confidence, respect, and openness—key components of effective, assertive communication.

The Foundation of Assertiveness

Assertiveness is grounded in self-assurance and respect for others. It's a balanced approach that allows us to express our thoughts, feelings, and needs directly and appropriately. Before we dive into specific gestures and postures, it's crucial to understand that the foundation of assertive body language is the mindset behind it. Feeling genuinely confident and valuing the person you're communicating with will naturally guide your body to reflect these attitudes.

Eye Contact: The Window to Confidence

Maintaining appropriate eye contact is perhaps the most critical aspect of assertive body language. It signifies attentiveness, honesty, and confidence. When speaking, aim for a balance—enough eye contact to show you're engaged but not so much that it feels confrontational. Similarly, when listening, eye contact demonstrates that you value the speaker's words. However, cultural nuances regarding eye contact should be respected; what's considered assertive in one culture may be perceived as aggressive in another.

Posture: Stand Your Ground, Openly

Your posture speaks volumes before you even utter a word. An assertive stance is upright and open, symbolizing confidence and readiness to engage. Slouching, in contrast, can appear uninterested or insecure, while an overly rigid posture might seem aggressive. Balance is key: stand or sit straight, relax your shoulders, and open your chest. This posture not only communicates assertiveness but also helps you feel more confident.

Gestures: The Harmony of Movement

Gestures can underscore the message you're trying to convey, adding emphasis and clarity. However, they should be natural and controlled. Excessive or frantic gestures might distract from your message or suggest nervousness. In assertive communication, use gestures to reinforce your points—like nodding to agree, using your hands to illustrate a concept, or showing your palms to indicate honesty and openness.

Facial Expressions: The Subtlety of Emotion

Your face reflects your emotions and attitudes, making facial expressions a powerful tool in assertive communication. A neutral or slightly positive facial expression can make you appear approachable and open to dialogue. Smiling genuinely, when appropriate, can ease tensions and foster a positive environment. However, be mindful of incongruence between your words and facial expressions, as this can lead to confusion or mistrust.

Spatial Awareness: Respecting Boundaries

Understanding and respecting personal space is essential in assertive communication. The distance you keep from someone can impact how your message is received. Too close might be intimidating, while too far could seem disinterested. The appropriate distance varies with cultural norms and individual comfort levels, but maintaining a respectful space is universally appreciated.

Vocal Tone: The Sound of Assertiveness

Although not strictly body language, your vocal tone complements your physical gestures and posture. An assertive tone is clear, steady, and moderate in volume—it conveys confidence without being overpowering. It's also important to match your tone with your message, ensuring your verbal and non-verbal cues are aligned.

Practicing Assertive Body Language

Incorporating assertive body language into your communication style takes practice and self-awareness. Begin by observing your own habits and gradually implementing changes. Remember, the goal is not to adopt a new persona but to communicate more effectively and authentically. Over time, these practices can become second nature, enhancing your interactions both personally and professionally.

Conclusion

Assertive body language is a vital component of effective communication. It reinforces your words, helping to convey your message clearly and confidently. By mastering the art of assertive body language—through eye contact, posture, gestures, facial expressions, spatial awareness, and vocal tone—you can enhance your ability to communicate assertively, fostering positive and respectful interactions in every aspect of your life.

NAVIGATING THE MAZE: GASLIGHTING AND THE POWER OF ASSERTIVENESS TRAINING

In the labyrinth of human interactions, two concepts stand in stark contrast yet often intersect in the journey towards personal empowerment: gaslighting and assertiveness training. This chapter delves into the intricate relationship between these two phenomena, exploring how assertiveness training can serve as a beacon of light, guiding individuals out of the fog cast by gaslighting.

Gaslighting: A Cloak of Confusion

Gaslighting, a term derived from the 1938 stage play "Gas Light," refers to a form of psychological manipulation in which a person seeks to sow seeds of doubt in a targeted individual or in members of a targeted group, making them question their own memory, perception, or judgment. This insidious tactic can lead to significant psychological distress, eroding the victim's sense of reality and self-confidence.

The effects of gaslighting are profoundly disorienting. Victims may find themselves constantly second-guessing their recollections and decisions, feeling a sense of general confusion and emotional turmoil. Over time, this can result in a crippling dependency on the gaslighter for validation and a distorted self-perception, making it challenging to assert one's needs, desires, and boundaries.

Assertiveness Training: The Path to Self-Assertion

In contrast, assertiveness training is a psychological therapy that aims to empower individuals to express their thoughts, feelings, and needs in a clear, honest, and respectful manner. It is rooted in the belief that everyone possesses the right to assert their personal boundaries without infringing on the rights of others.

Assertiveness training equips individuals with the tools to recognize and assert their rights, communicate effectively, and handle conflict constructively. Through various techniques and exercises, participants learn to express themselves confidently and to stand up for themselves in a healthy, balanced way.

The Intersection: From Gaslighting to Empowerment

The intersection of gaslighting and assertiveness training is a crucial battleground in the fight for personal autonomy and psychological well-being. For those ensnared in the web of gaslighting, assertiveness training offers a way out—a means to reclaim their voice and agency.

1. Recognizing Gaslighting: The first step in this journey is recognizing the presence of gaslighting. Assertiveness training provides individuals with the awareness to identify manipulative behaviors and understand their impact on one's sense of self.

2. Building Self-Confidence: Central to assertiveness training is the development of self-confidence. This is vital for victims of gaslighting, as it helps rebuild the self-esteem that has been eroded by ongoing manipulation.

3. Developing Communication Skills: Effective communication is a cornerstone of assertiveness training. For those affected by gaslighting, learning to express their thoughts and feelings clearly and directly is essential in countering manipulation and establishing boundaries.

4. Setting Boundaries: Assertiveness training emphasizes the importance of setting and maintaining personal boundaries. This skill is particularly empowering for gaslighting victims, as it enables them to protect their mental and emotional well-being from further manipulation.

5. Empowerment Through Practice: The journey from victimhood to empowerment is gradual and requires practice. Assertiveness training offers a safe space for individuals to practice their newfound skills, gain confidence, and reinforce their commitment to self-respect and personal integrity.

In conclusion, while gaslighting seeks to diminish and disorient, assertiveness training shines as a tool for empowerment and recovery. By fostering self-awareness, building confidence, and honing communication skills, assertiveness training enables individuals to navigate out of the shadows of gaslighting and into the light of self-assuredness and personal freedom. In this journey, the ultimate destination is not just the ability to assert oneself but the realization of one's inherent worth and the unassailable right to live free from manipulation and control.

PEOPLE PLEASERS

In psychology, people who habitually strive to please others or seek approval are often referred to as "people pleasers." This term is commonly used in both professional and casual contexts to describe individuals who prioritize others' needs and desires over their own, often to their own detriment.

The behavior of a people pleaser can be linked to several psychological concepts, including:

1. Codependency: This is a behavioral condition where a person excessively cares for others' needs at the expense of their own. It's often seen in relationships where one person enables another's immaturity, irresponsibility, or underachievement.

2. Low Self-Esteem: People pleasers often have underlying issues with self-esteem. They might believe that their worth is tied to how much they can do for others or how well they can keep others happy.

3. Fear of Rejection or Abandonment: People pleasers might act the way they do out of fear that they will be disliked, rejected, or abandoned if they do not meet others' expectations or needs.

4. Attachment Issues: Early experiences in life, especially those related to attachment to primary caregivers, can influence people-pleasing behaviors. Insecure attachment styles may contribute to a heightened need to please others to maintain relationships.

5. Conflict Avoidance: People pleasers often avoid conflict at all costs. They believe that agreeing with others and not expressing their true feelings or needs will keep the peace.

It's important to recognize that being considerate and accommodating is not inherently negative. However, people-pleasing becomes a concern when it consistently overrides one's own needs and leads to stress, burnout, or being taken advantage of. Therapy and self-help strategies can be effective in addressing these patterns and fostering a healthier balance in relationships.

NAVIGATING THE PSYCHOLOGICAL MAZE

The Intricate Web of Gaslighting

Gaslighting, a form of psychological manipulation, undermines the victim's reality, causing them to question their perceptions, memories, and even sanity. This subtle yet devastating tactic can have profound implications on one's mental health, fostering an environment where the victim becomes excessively dependent on external validation and approval.

The Quest for External Validation

In the shadow of gaslighting, individuals often find themselves in a relentless pursuit of external validation. This insatiable need arises from the manipulator's constant questioning and devaluation of the victim's experiences and feelings, leading to a deep-seated insecurity. The victim, desperate to re-establish their shaken sense of reality, turns outward, seeking affirmation from others to validate their worth and perceptions.

External Approval: A Double-Edged Sword

Seeking approval from others is a natural human inclination; it becomes problematic when it turns into a compulsive need. In the context of gaslighting, this need is amplified, pushing the individual to constantly seek reassurance from external sources. While momentarily gratifying, this dependence can erode self-esteem, as the individual's sense of value becomes contingent on the fluctuating opinions and validation of others.

Assertiveness: A Shield Against Manipulation

Assertiveness stands as a beacon of strength amid the chaos wrought by gaslighting. It is the ability to express one's thoughts, feelings, and needs in a straightforward, honest, and respectful manner. More than a communication skill, assertiveness is a defense mechanism that empowers individuals to set boundaries, reject manipulation, and reclaim their sense of self.

The Role of Assertiveness

Assertiveness serves multiple roles in counteracting the effects of gaslighting:

Boundary Setting: It enables individuals to define and communicate their limits clearly, protecting them from further manipulation.

Self-Advocacy: Assertiveness encourages individuals to advocate for their needs and interests, fostering a sense of autonomy and self-respect.

Reality Anchoring: By confidently asserting their perceptions and experiences, victims can begin to trust their reality again, reducing the need for external validation.

Cultivating Assertiveness

Developing assertiveness involves introspection, practice, and patience. It begins with understanding one's rights and recognizing the value of one's needs and feelings. Assertiveness training often includes techniques for expressing oneself effectively, such as using "I" statements, practicing active listening, and learning to manage conflict constructively.

Conclusion

Gaslighting, by eroding the victim's sense of reality, fosters an unhealthy dependence on external validation and approval. Assertiveness emerges as a critical defense mechanism, offering a pathway to reclaiming one's voice and sense of self. Through assertiveness, individuals can establish healthy boundaries, advocate for their needs, and, ultimately, break free from the cycle of manipulation and validation seeking. This journey towards assertiveness is not just about combating gaslighting; it is about embracing one's worth, fostering resilience, and cultivating a profound sense of self-trust and authenticity.

THE HUMAN PSYCHE

The human psyche, a complex and multifaceted entity, is understood through various psychological perspectives, each offering unique insights into our mental and emotional makeup. These perspectives, like psychoanalysis, Jungian analysis, and modern understandings of trauma, contribute to a more holistic understanding of human behavior and mental health.

Psychoanalysis and the Unconscious Mind

Psychoanalysis, pioneered by Sigmund Freud, delves into the unconscious mind. It emphasizes the impact of early childhood experiences and the role of subconscious drives and desires in shaping behavior. Key concepts like repression, defense mechanisms, and Freud's theory of the mind's structure (id, ego, superego) have significantly influenced our understanding of human behavior, even as some of Freud's ideas have been challenged or revised over time.

Jungian Psychology and Archetypes

Carl Jung, a contemporary of Freud, developed his own approach, focusing on the collective unconscious and archetypes. Jung believed that universal, archetypal symbols exist in a collective unconscious shared by all humans. This perspective highlights the role of myths, dreams, and symbols in understanding the human psyche. Jungian analysis is particularly influential in the realms of dream interpretation and understanding personality types.

Trauma and Modern Psychological Perspectives

Modern psychology has broadened the understanding of trauma, particularly in how experiences like gaslighting or prolonged exposure to negative suggestions can impact mental health. The study of trauma emphasizes the body's psychological and physiological responses to overwhelming events, reshaping the understanding of disorders like PTSD. This perspective is crucial in developing effective treatments for trauma survivors, emphasizing the need for compassionate, trauma-informed care.

Integrating Multiple Perspectives for a Holistic Understanding

No single psychological perspective fully encapsulates the complexities of the human psyche. Integrating multiple viewpoints, from psychoanalysis to trauma-informed approaches, allows for a more nuanced understanding of human behavior and mental processes. This integration is crucial for effective psychological treatment and for advancing our understanding of the human condition.

In conclusion, the various schools of psychology, each with their unique lenses, collectively contribute to a more comprehensive understanding of the human psyche. Whether it's exploring the depths of the unconscious, interpreting symbolic dreams, or addressing the impacts of trauma, these perspectives together enrich our comprehension of the intricate tapestry of the human mind.

THE INTERSECTION OF SELF AND SPIRIT: UNDERSTANDING OUR INNER BATTLES

In the journey of self-discovery and personal growth, we often find ourselves at the crossroads of psychology and spirituality. This chapter delves into the intricate relationship between our inner psychological battles and our spiritual quests, particularly focusing on the phenomena of gaslighting, the pursuit of external validation, and their spiritual implications.

Gaslighting, a term rooted in psychological discourse, describes a form of emotional manipulation where an individual is made to doubt their own reality. This insidious technique not only undermines one's sense of self but also **erodes their confidence**, leading to a profound sense of disconnection from their inner truth. In a world where external validation is frequently sought to compensate for internal voids, this manipulation becomes especially detrimental.

But what happens when we view this struggle through a spiritual lens? In many spiritual traditions, the essence of our being is closely tied to our understanding and respect for a higher power or divine principle. <u>When we lose touch with our inner selves, as often happens under the shadow of gaslighting, we might unknowingly drift away from this divine connection.</u> **The relentless pursuit of external validation is akin to the worship of false idols,** a concept prevalent in various spiritual teachings. **These 'idols', whether they be the approval of others, material success,** or superficial relationships, offer only fleeting satisfaction, **leaving a deeper void within.**

This chapter explores how the neglect of our spiritual selves in favor of these external 'idols' can lead us into a metaphorical hell - **a state of perpetual dissatisfaction and disconnection from our true nature.** It invites readers to reflect on their own experiences and consider how their psychological struggles might be mirrored in their spiritual lives.

Moreover, this chapter offers insights into how **reconnecting with our spiritual essence can provide a path to healing from psychological wounds.** It discusses practices from various traditions that emphasize introspection, mindfulness, and the cultivation of **a relationship with the divine as ways to foster self-esteem and a sense of inner peace.**

As we navigate the complex interplay of our psychological and spiritual selves, it's crucial to approach our journey with empathy, open-mindedness, and a willingness to explore the depths of our being. This chapter aims to be a **guiding light for those seeking to understand the intersection of their psychological struggles with their souls.**

ASSERTIVE COMMUNICATION EXAMPLES

A ssertive communication involves expressing oneself in a direct, respectful, and honest way while considering the feelings and rights of others. Here are some examples:
Expressing Opinions: "I believe we should consider more options before making a decision. This approach seems limited."

Refusing Requests: "I understand you need help with the project, but I can't commit to this right now due to my current workload."

Setting Boundaries: "I appreciate your interest in my personal life, but I prefer keeping work and private matters separate."

Providing Feedback: "Your presentation was very informative, but I think adding more data would make your argument stronger."

Requesting Change: "I've noticed you often interrupt me during meetings. Could we work on a way that allows everyone to speak uninterrupted?"

Negotiating: "I understand your perspective, but let's find a middle ground that benefits both our departments."

Acknowledging Mistakes: "I realize I missed the deadline, and I apologize for the inconvenience. I've taken steps to ensure it doesn't happen again."

Addressing Conflicts: "I feel upset when my ideas are dismissed without discussion. Can we talk about a way to communicate our opinions more effectively?"

These examples show how assertive communication can be used in various situations while maintaining respect and clarity.

ASSERTIVENESS TRAINING EXAMPLES: WORK AND FAMILY

Assertiveness training involves practical exercises designed to improve communication skills, enhance self-esteem, and empower individuals to express their needs and desires confidently and respectfully. This chapter presents ten examples each for work and family contexts, illustrating how assertiveness can be effectively applied to navigate common scenarios.

Assertiveness in the Workplace

Requesting Feedback: "I've noticed I haven't received much feedback on my recent project. Could we schedule a meeting to discuss your thoughts and any areas for improvement?"

Declining Additional Work When Overloaded: "I understand the importance of this new project, but I'm currently at capacity with my existing commitments. Can we discuss priorities or delegate some tasks to ensure the quality of work isn't compromised?"

Addressing a Missed Promotion: "I was hopeful about the recent promotion opportunity and would like to understand the decision-making process. Could we discuss what skills or experiences I should focus on to be considered in the future?"

Negotiating a Raise: "I've contributed to several successful projects this year and taken on additional responsibilities. I'd like to discuss the possibility of a salary adjustment to reflect my contributions to the team."

Handling Criticism: "I appreciate your feedback and understand your concerns. Could we explore specific examples so I can better understand how to improve?"

Setting Boundaries for Work-Life Balance: "To maintain productivity and well-being, I propose setting clear boundaries regarding work hours and communication outside of those hours. Let's discuss a plan that respects everyone's personal time."

Requesting Resources for a Project: "This project has the potential to significantly impact our goals. To ensure its success, I need additional resources. Can we review what's available and how to allocate them effectively?"

Addressing Unprofessional Behavior: "The comments made during the meeting were not only hurtful to me but also unprofessional. Let's discuss how we can communicate in a respectful and constructive manner."

Asking for Flexible Working Arrangements: "Given my current circumstances, I believe a flexible working arrangement could improve my productivity and work-life balance. Can we explore options that could work for both of us?"

Initiating a Difficult Conversation: "I've noticed some tension between us lately and it's affecting our collaboration. Can we set aside some time to talk about it and find a way to work together more effectively?"

Assertiveness in the Family

Discussing Household Responsibilities: "I've noticed I've been taking on the majority of household chores. Can we discuss a more balanced way to share these tasks?"

Setting Boundaries with Relatives: "While we appreciate your advice and concern, we need to make decisions that are best for our family. Let's discuss how we can respect each other's boundaries."

Addressing Financial Contributions: "As we're all benefiting from living together, it's important we discuss everyone's financial contribution to household expenses."

Negotiating Curfews with Teenagers: "I understand your desire for more independence, but I'm concerned for your safety. Let's find a curfew time that works for both of us."

Managing Screen Time for Children: "Let's talk about the amount of screen time that's appropriate. We want to ensure there's a good balance with other activities."

Planning Family Activities: "I've noticed we have different interests in activities. Let's come up with a plan that includes activities everyone can enjoy."

Addressing Behavior Issues: "When you do [specific behavior], it makes me feel [specific feeling]. Can we talk about what's going on and how we can work together to improve the situation?"

Discussing Educational Choices: "I understand your perspective on choosing a college, but it's also important to consider all factors, including finances and career prospects. Let's discuss all options openly."

Handling Disputes Among Siblings: "I see that there's a disagreement here. Let's each take a turn to explain our side without interruption, and then we can look for a solution together."

Communicating Personal Needs: "Lately, I've been feeling overwhelmed and need some time for self-care. Can we discuss how we can support each other in taking personal time?"

These examples illustrate how assertiveness can be applied in both work and family contexts to address challenges, improve relationships, and foster a healthy, respectful environment. The key is to communicate openly, listen actively, and seek mutually beneficial solutions.

Printed in Great Britain
by Amazon